hodge podge

"powerful proverbs"

By

charles B. hodge

Published By
BIBLICAL RESEARCH PRESS
774 East North 15th Street
Abilene, Texas
79601

HODGE PODGE

by

Charles B. Hodge

◆

Copyright © 1969, by

BIBLICAL RESEARCH PRESS

◆

Library of Congress Catalog Card No. 71-92047

◆

PREFACE

We all appreciate Proverbs! Catchy phrases and statements that convey meaningful truth are both intriguing and pleasant.

Particularly ministers and editors of church bulletins or other types of journals find these gems of wisdom helpful in communicating brief pointed lessons and provoking both serious and humorous thought.

We have been using *Hodgepodge* (a play on my name) for over sixteen years in our local church bulletin and its use has become a conversation topic, even outside the congregation. Finally, the demand has come for us to publish "The Best of Hodgepodge" in a form that will allow for wider usefulness and enjoyment and, we hope, make many others happier and at the same time more spiritual. We have therefore classified and categorized the statements and edited them carefully and now we send them forth hoping that they will provoke honest thinking and challenge nobility and will even produce hearty chuckles.

Charles B. Hodge

CONTENTS

CHARACTER

You can tell what a man is by what he does when he hasn't anything to do.

I am a *Fool for Christ's Sake*—whose fool are you?

The *yoke of God* does not fit *stiff necks*.

Opportunity has to knock; temptation only to stand outside and whistle.

> There comes to me these questions
> With searching, sincere cry!
> "Through storms of life and struggles
> How well—and what—teach I?"

When you are through changing—you're through.

Man is the only man that blushes—or needs to.—Mark Twain.

Nothing is so full of victory as patience.

A test of any man's character is how he takes praise.

Unless there is *WITHIN* us that which is *ABOVE* us, we will soon yield to that which is *ABOUT* us, and sink into that which is *BENEATH* us.

By the time one is old enough to know better, he thinks he is smart enough not to be caught at it.

When you flee temptation, don't leave a forwarding address.

As we grow better we meet better people.

If we could see ourselves as others—we'd deny it!

Your character is built with what you stand for; your reputation by what you fall for.

Attitude not altitude gets one to heaven.

Patience is the ability to idle your motor when you wish to strip your gears.

You must climb the mountain if you wish to view the plain.

Half the problems that come in Christianity come in half living it.

2

When you are just average you are as close to the bottom as the top.

Christianity is the best armor but the worst cloak.

All sunshine makes a desert.

Christianity is a battle—not a dream.

Gifts are what a man has—graces are what a man is.

What most of us need is more horsepower and less exhaust.

People who deserve a monument do not need one.

The first 40 years of a man's life is text, the next 30 years the commentary.

The trouble with singing your own praises—you always pitch it too high.

It's that little difference in each of us that is the big difference.

Temper improves the longer you keep it.

When a man gets too big for his breeches, his hat doesn't fit either.

Conscience is something inside that bothers you when nothing outside does.

Judge a man not by his worth but what is worth imitating.

One day I shall be what I am becoming.

Understanding others changes us.

Life is tons of discipline.—Frost.

It is not how old you are but how you are old.

Every man over 40 is responsible for his face.

Character is not made in a crisis—it is only exhibited.—Dr. Freeman.

The best victory is self-conquest.

"Wild oats" take something out of the soil of man's life that no crop rotation can restore.

"When a man comes to borrow from me," said the banker, "the best security is character. If he doesn't have it, he's a bad risk, regardless of collateral."

Nudity may cause some women to be chased but not chaste.

Life is too short to be little.

Man has learned to fly like a bird and swim like a fish—he just needs to learn to live like a man.

God will not look you over for medals, degrees, or diplomas—but for scars.—Hubbard.

Keep your temper—no one else wants it.

The man false to God will not be true to anyone.

Character is caught as well as taught.

We see things not as they are but as we are.

Character is a victory—not a gift.

A withered soul in a healthy body is only a live corpse.

The bigger a man's head gets, the easier to fill his shoes.

When a man feels the world owes him a living he is usually too lazy to collect it.

It is better to be great in your littleness than little in your greatness.

No matter what your life on earth is—build something on it.

No one worth possessing can be possessed.

Character is what a man is in the dark.

The man who stresses "his rights" usually wants to do wrong.

We are a part of all we met.—Tennyson.

The man who wakes up to find himself great has not been asleep.

4

To be yourself, forget yourself.

Imagination was given to man to compensate him for what he is not . . . and a sense of humor to console him for what he is.

Courageous Christians conquer conflicts.

Many have "ability" but no "stability."

The right attitude is to do a thing when you have the wrong attitude.

Humility makes a man feel smaller as he becomes greater.

The best tranquilizer is a clear conscience.

Sorrow makes one "bitter" or "better."

Shine the heels of your shoes as well as the toes.

Nerve is nerves controlled.

Reputation is like a bubble—it may burst if you puff it up too high.

A man's best boss is a well trained conscience.

All great men had weaknesses, but no weak man ever achieved greatness.

CHILDREN

One important way for us to help our children grow up is for us to grow up first.

Some parents could do more for their children by not doing so much for them.

Usually parents who are lucky in the kind of children they have, have children who are lucky in the kind of parents they have.

Sometimes the best way to straighten out a youngster is by bending him over.

Some fathers worry more about their "golf swing" than their "off spring."

The best thing you can spend on your children is your time.

CHURCH SIGN "Be the soul supporter of your children."

An adolescent is one who, when not treated as an adult, acts like an infant.

Weeds and grain grow in the same field; the only difference is their parents.

Children are like airplanes; you only hear of the ones that crashed.

Why can't life's problems hit at 18 when we know all the answers.

Parents are baby-sitters for God.

It is unthinkable to expect a child to listen to your advice, and ignore your example.

Understanding the atom is child's play compared with child's play.

"Be home by 10:00." "I'm no longer a child." "That's why you be home by 10:00."

When children get on the wrong track it is time to use the switch.

Many of us are out fighting fires when our children are home playing with matches.

One of the first things one notices in backward countries— kids still obey their parents.

Men build the road but women teach children to walk on them.

The devil first makes friends with parents to get their boys and girls.

Give to a pig when it grunts and a child when it cries and you will have a good pig and a bad child.

Sometimes a "big gun" at the office isn't even a "pop" at home.

If we paid no more attention to our plants than we do our children we would live in a jungle.

If you wish to follow in your father's footsteps, don't wear loafers.

It's hard for a child to live right when he has never seen it done.

There are too many fathers who tie up the dog at night and turn the children loose.

If you are interested in how your child turns out, be interested when he turns in.

One reason children are seen on the streets so much at night— they are afraid to be home alone.

He who cannot control his youth will not enjoy his old age.

The best way to bring up children is to never let them down.

The proper place to stop crime is in the "high chair" not the "electric chair."

Spare the Freud and save the child.

A baby has a way of making a man out of his Daddy and a boy of his Grandfather.

Bear in mind that children of all ages have one thing in common—they close their ears to advice and open their eyes to example.

The more one grows up, the less one blows up.

You have to do your own growing no matter how tall your grandfather was.

CHURCH

When a church no longer reaches out, it passes out.

Don't worry about woodpeckers on the outside; worry about the termites inside.

Church Sign "Be a space traveler—begin here."

Church Sign "Redemption Center—No Stamps Needed."

Preacher in baptistry, "I hope I have a tither in the tank."

Folks not identified are like hens who eat here and lay elsewhere.

If absence does make the heart grow fonder, some really must love the church.

Why don't men who dislike the church move to where there is not one?

> The church is near,
> But the road is icy—
> The tavern is far
> But I'll drive carefully!

Churches have three kinds of members—pickers, kickers, and stickers.

Education is a working chest of tools.

Some members sing "Standing on the Promises" while "sitting on the premises."

The extent of some people's religion is knowing the name of the church they stay away from.

God shook the world with a babe—not a bomb.

If you missed the last Sunday on earth you will miss the first Sunday in heaven.

So you are as good as half the church—which half?

The greatest cross in life is to be without a cross.

The church cannot win its way in the world following the ways of the world.

A Christian's duty is as plain as A-B-C; trouble is, many are D-E-F.

Rootage is necessary for fruitage.

Two things make Americans mad: 1) to hear Christianity criticized, and 2) to see Christianity practiced.

We are not Seventh Day Adventists but first day absentists.

Some church members are like the farmer's well—in the winter they freeze up and in the summer they dry up.

Some bright children should be applauded with one hand.

Christians are like pianos—grand, square, and upright—and no good out of tune.

We will never bring the world unto Christ until we bring Christ to the world.

Christianity is like an airplane—when you stop you drop.

The fellow always talking hypocrites in the church has a taste for buzzard.

If you want the church to go—go to church.

A good time to be religious is when you don't feel like it.

It's hard to sell a product you don't use and religion you don't live.

Many find the church cold because they sit on the "Z" row seat.

The church is made of willing members; some willing to work and the others willing to let them.

A cold church like cold butter does not spread well.

If you want to know how popular the preacher is, come Sunday morning. If you want to know how popular the church is, come Sunday night. If you want to know how popular Christ is, come Wednesday night.

We don't believe in instrumental music in worship but too many of us "fiddle around" in church work.

Church members ought to show others how to live—not criticize them for not knowing.

Folks are quick to condemn a man who does wrong—unless he is a church member—then they condemn the church.

Have a heart and save a soul.

Revive the church—begin with me.

The loss of Christian character is usually prophesied by absence from service.

Your religion must be *intense* before it can be *extensive*.

Who ever preferred to drown rather than getting into a boat with a hypocrite?

Judging by the way some church members live, they need fire insurance.

If the entire church would work like a faction we could take the world for Christ.

The church is a work-shop for wide-awake Christians—not a dormitory for sleeping ones.

The world at its worst needs the church at its best.

I am not worried about the church in the world as I am about the world in the church.

Some members worry more about the state of the world than the state of the church.

Everyone in the church
The church in everyone.

It takes the whole church
To take the whole truth
To the whole world.

When a church member rests he rusts.

Some brethren know more about *profit* than the *prophets*.

Many want the Christ of the cross without the cross of Christ.

Many who go to church the most worship the least.

Some members are like a tire with a slow leak—it takes a lot of pumping to keep them inflated.

> Coming together is a beginning;
> Keeping together is progress;
> Working together is success.

It's a great day when empty sinners and a full Christ meet.

Recently a church fired its preacher. The reason—2 years ago they told him to begin evening services. They found out last week he hadn't.

Many think of the church like a hospital. They really don't want to go but they're glad it's there when they have to.

Some divorce the church then look for alimony.

Religion is what you do *for people* not *to people*.

Satan is never too busy to rock the cradle of a sleeping Christian.

Church attendance is determined more by desire than distance.

Quitters in the church are like motors—they sputter before they miss and miss before they quit.

The less religion a church has the more entertainment it takes to get them there.

You don't lose religion like a blow-out but with a slow leak.

People say, "I don't like revivals—they don't last." Well, neither does a bath.

Sunday church will not convert the sinners you cheated all week.

You need the church—the church needs you—the world needs both.

You cannot *PUSH* the Bible school without *"U"* in it.

To grow the church must have knee power and shoe leather.

Are elders to "oversee" or "overlook"?

A church that is always chewing the rag isn't well fed.

Gloomy church folks are the ones who pay more attention to the "don'ts" than the "do's."

Some wish to be counted "in" but not counted "on."

Religion is a process to be repeated—not recalled.

Song after prayer, " 'Tis so sweet to rust in Jesus."

A closed church means an open town.

EDUCATION

Education makes people easy to lead but difficult to drive; easy to govern but impossible to enslave.

A learned man always carries his wealth with him.

A clever devil is more dangerous than a dumb one—there were intellects behind the Nazi movement—there are brains in communism. We need brains, yes, but actually we need character.

Many a man thinks he has an open mind when it's merely vacant.

We are all ignorant. We are just ignorant about different things.—Will Rogers.

Your stomach can be full but not your mind.

Most of us think we think.

Imagination is sometimes better than knowledge.

Honest failure is a necessary part of learning.

An educated fool is a bigger one than an ignorant one.

A person gets paid for using his brains—not having them.

Knowledge is proud it knows so much; wisdom is humble it knows so little.

An expert is one who knows more and more about less and less.

It takes only a little squirt to imagine himself the fountain of wisdom.

The badge of intelligence is the question mark.

It takes a lot to teach a little.

Ideas are funny things—they won't work unless you do.

Some drink deeply from the fountain of knowledge; others just gargle.

The school of experience is post-graduate work.

There is only one thing more expensive than education—ignorance.

Big men know they are big; little men think they are big.

What you don't know you can learn.

The human mind was intended for a storehouse not a wastebasket.

A man who knows all the answers has likely been running around with questionable folk.

The highest education is to learn to do God's will.

Many seem allergic to food for thought.

Lincoln was great, not because he lived in a log cabin, but because he got out of it.

He is educated who is most useful.

Reading the fine print will give you an education—not reading it will give you experience.

ENTHUSIASM

Enthusiasm is as contagious as the measles and as powerful as dynamite.

Every man is enthusiastic as times. Some 30 minutes, others 30 hours, but the one who has it 30 years makes a success.

If you can give your son but one gift, make it enthusiasm.

Better for a pot to boil over than never boil.

The mosquito never gets a slap on the back until he goes to work.

The best applause comes from your conscience.

No man is dead broke who has five senses.

Give people a piece of your heart rather than a piece of your mind.

I would rather lose in a cause that someday will win than win in a cause that someday will lose.

Everything comes to him who hustles while he waits.

Saints are sinners who kept on trying.

The difficult is done immediately; the impossible takes a little longer.

Weakness of men: "catch trouble by the horns and opportunity by the tail."

It's not wildfire that worries me in the church—it is no fire.

None are as old as those who have outlived enthusiasm.

The kind of religion that makes men look sick cannot cure the world.

He who has no fire in himself cannot warm others.

There is no "I" in "team."

Nothing great was ever accomplished without enthusiasm.

If you cannot win at least make the fellow ahead of you break the record.

A pessimist is one who feels bad when he feels good for fear he will feel worse when he feels better.

I prefer the mistakes of enthusiasm to the indifference of wisdom.

Trying times is no reason to quit trying.

EXCUSES

An excuse is a thin skin of falsehood stretched tightly over a baldfaced lie.

Excuses may satisfy you but not save you.

Even peace can be purchased at too high a price.—Benjamin Franklin.

You can catch a man without money, sometimes without tobacco, but never without an excuse.

"*U*" are in every exc*u*se!

Small deeds done are better than big deeds only planned.

A man who has no will to get ahead need not leave a will behind.

You could get rich manufacturing crutches for lame excuses.

January 2nd is when people find it easier to break a resolution than a habit.

The man who honestly tries can never be counted a failure.

Many try to find peace in a pill.

There are three stages in American history. The passing of the Indian, the passing of the buffalo, and the passing of the buck.—Will Rogers.

One reason dollar bills wear out so quickly is because so many folks pass the buck.

Adam used 15 words to tell of Eve's sin, and only 3 for his own.

Too many reach for the stool when there is a piano to be moved.

It is a big thing to do small things well.

God gives birds their food but they must fly for it.

Good ancestors are no excuse for being sorry.

Following the line of least resistance makes both rivers and men crooked.

When religion gets in past tense it becomes pretense.

Kind words may never die, but without kind deeds they sound mighty sick.

You cannot plow a field by merely turning it over in your mind.

Some rise to the occasion—others merely go up in the air.

When the road is straight—don't look for a short cut.

With every sin the devil provides also an excuse.

Folks who saved for a rainy day are deluged by drips who didn't.

Souls cost soles.

A poor excuse never made a contribution to a worthy cause.

EXPERIENCE

One reason experience is such a good teacher—she doesn't allow dropouts.

Training is learning the rules; experience the exceptions.

Experience is what you get while you are trying to avoid it.

It takes a baby two years to learn to talk and 60 years to keep its mouth shut.

Humility is the ability to be ashamed when people tell you how wonderful you are.

No one can make a fool of us—this is our prerogative.

Many hurry to catch up—few to get ahead.

The great use of life is to spend it on something that outlasts it.

Experience is that which recognizes a mistake the second time around.

Finding a way to live the simple life today is man's most complicated task.

A man should never be ashamed of saying he has been in the wrong; this means he knows more today than yesterday.

It is buried seed that grows—not buried talents.

It is a costly wisdom purchased by experience.

You always know which people have found a bed of roses—you hear them complaining about the thorns.

Experience is what you get when you expect something else.

A man can stand in his own poverty better than he can stand on other's prosperity.

Better a blush on the face than a blot in the heart.—Cervantes.

Regret is insight that arrived too late.

The function of fear is to warn us of danger, not to make us afraid to face it.

It is difficult to see the picture when you are inside the frame.

The man who leads the band must turn his back on the crowd.

FAITH

Faith ends when worry begins; worry ends when faith begins.

An atheist cannot find God for the same reason a thief cannot find a policeman.

Nothing is so firmly believed as what is least known.— Montaigne.

Feed your faith and your doubts will starve to death.

Ulcers are the result of mountain climbing over molehills.

Faith sees the invisible, believes the incredible, and achieves the impossible.

When a man wants to believe something, it doesn't take much to convince him.

Fear freezes but faith thaws.

When a belief rests upon nothing you cannot knock away the foundations.—William Yeats.

You cannot walk with God running with the devil.

If Christ is kept outside, something is wrong inside.

Faith keeps a man that keeps his faith.

I do not merely wish to possess a faith; I want a faith that possesses me.

If our faith cannot move mountains, it ought to at least climb them.

FORGIVENESS

It's easier to forgive an enemy than a friend.

Faults are thick where love is thin.

The person who looks up to God seldom looks down on man.

Sympathy is *your* pain in *my* heart.

The envied, when living, are praised when dead.

You may have a "heart of pure gold" but so does a hard boiled egg.

To forgive our enemies their virtues—that is a greater miracle. —Voltaire.

He who cannot forgive destroys the bridge over which he also must pass.

A man's venom poisons himself more than its victim.

You cannot do kindness too soon, because you never know how soon it will be too late.

Sympathy is two hearts tugging at the same load.

We are always too busy to visit the sick but never too busy to serve as pall-bearer.

The test of courage comes when in the minority; the test of tolerance when in the majority.

He who forgives ends the quarrel.

The less tenderness a man has, the more is required in others.

No one can go to heaven who wants to go alone.

Often we feel guilty for what we did but seldom for what we are.

Where we are wrong makes us willing to change; where we are right makes us easy to live with.

Forgiveness saves the expense of anger, the cost of hatred, and the waste of energy.

FRIENDSHIP

The world is round so that friendship may circle it.

Real friends are those, when you have made a fool of yourself, don't conclude it is a permanent job.

The enemies a man makes by taking a stand generally respect him more than the friends he made sitting on the fence.

A friend you have to buy is not worth what you paid for him.

A true friend thinks you are still a good egg when half cracked.

Your friend would not look so dirty if you cleaned your glasses.

All smoke the pipe of peace but none inhale.

When you pass out the milk of human kindness don't skim it.

The only way to have a friend is to be one.

Am I my brother's keeper? No, but I am my brother's brother.

Steel that loses its temper is worthless.

Our best investment is not in funds but friends.

It is easy to flatter but hard to praise.

Kindness is the oil which takes much of the friction out of life.

Tact is making your friends feel at home when you wish they were.

Friendship is a vitamin—"B-1."

The strongest words are used in the weakest arguments.

No matter how much you nurse a grudge it will not get better.

The most inflammable wood is a chip on your shoulder.

Any man can stand up before his enemies; give me a man who can stand up before his friends.—Gladstone.

You can make more friends in 2 months being interested in others than in 2 years trying to get them interested in you.

Pick your friends—but not to pieces.

If you were another person would you be a friend of yourself?

The hardest to love needs our love the most.

We like the man who comes out and says what he thinks—when he agrees with us.

I prefer burnt toast to hot tongue.

Porcupines are never petted.

It is better to offer a hand than point a finger.

A man is also known by the people he doesn't keep.

Getting even puts you on his level.

Science has made the world a neighborhood but only Christ can make it a brotherhood.

The best way to get rid of an enemy is to make a friend of him.

The slanderer sometimes is less dangerous than the flatterer.

Friends—Two women who are mad at the same person.

Try to spell "brothers" without "others."

When someone makes a mistake rub it "out" not "in."

The continuing battles of life are between men and their enemies and between women and their friends.

Some take you for what you are; others take you for what you have; the rest simply can't take you.

The secret of popularity is to treat adults like kids and kids like adults.

We too often love things and use people when we should be using things and loving people.

GIVING

You used to couldn't take it with you—now you cannot even leave it behind.

It's OK to itch for things if you are willing to scratch for them.

You can make a good living yet live a poor life.

What you do with your money determines what your money will do to you.

When money is found on trees some grafting is going on.

A pig bought on credit grunts all year.

They who think money will do anything will do anything for money.

You say money talks? Introduce it to God!

The real measure of wealth is how much we would be worth if we lost it.

Who gives to me teaches me to give.

A fat purse will not compensate for a lean soul.

Some spend money they don't have to buy things they don't need to fool folks they don't like.

The poorest man is he who only has money.—Rockefeller.

Giving is true having.

"Old brother Horner, sat in a corner, as the contribution passed by. Sweetly content, he dropped in a cent, and said: 'What a fine Christian am I.' "

What if the Lord made us as poor as our giving shows?

If you make the church important, it is quite likely to return the favor.

Too many, in the fight against the devil, will give no quarter, no not one.

Many give a tenth to the Lord—a tenth of what they should give.

The way some give is living proof *little things count.*

The only thing Christ left on earth was his blood.

> Who gives of wealth gives little else—
> Who gives of love gives all.
> The former shrinks to nothingness,
> The latter grows straight and tall.

Some give their mite; some give with all their might; and some don't give who might.

A man who lives for himself is ruined by the company he keeps.

The time to save money is when you have some to save.

When it comes to giving—some stop at nothing.

Today believers *BUY* and cannot *GIVE*; New Testament Christians *SOLD* where they could give.

The quickest way to lose your shirt is to put too much on the cuff.

The hardest thing to give is . . . . . *IN!*

About all you can do with money these days is owe it.

If you wish to see what God thinks of money look at those he has given it to.

> It isn't what I would do
>   If a million should fall my lot;
> But what I am doing today
>   With the dollar and quarter I've got!

Cheap giving is cheap living.

Everything in the world can be endured except continual prosperity.—Goethe.

An ungrateful man is like a hog eating acorns under the trees yet never looking up to see where they came from.

Being poor is a problem but being rich is not the answer.

Love is not "intense" until it bears "expense."

Don't cheat the Lord and call it economy.

Beggars can be choosers these days.

Complete possession is only proved by giving. All you are unable to give possesses you.

The rich stay rich by pretending to be poor; the poor stay poor by pretending to be rich.

What you don't owe won't hurt you.

A spendthrift is a man who turns his heirs gray.

GOSSIP

Do not remove a fly from one's head with a hatchet.

It isn't necessary to blow the other fellow's light out to let yours shine.

When some put in their *two cents worth* they have some change coming.

Gossip, claiming to have eyes, is as blind as a bat.

Gossip is like a balloon—it grows bigger with every puff.

If so many people were not so glad to carry it, gossip could not travel very far.

Some use the tongue to express thought, to conceal thought, or instead of thought.

He says so many things out of line he should be arrested for *jay talking*.

The bad you hear about a man may not be true, but when people say something good about him you can bet on it.

He only opens his mouth to change feet.

GOSSIP—"Letting the 'chat' out of the bag."

The man who talks about his brother to you will talk about you to his brother.

People who gossip usually wind up in their own *mouth traps*.

Gossip—"Have tale, will tattle."

> Gossip is a little insect,
>   It has neither legs nor wings.
> It is made up wholly of *tales*
>   And most of them have stings.

Slander has to be bad to be good.

A whale gets *harpooned* only when *spouting*.

Those who tell *little white lies* soon become color blind.

Some find fault as if it were buried treasure.

People, like cats, lick themselves with their tongues.

It is much easier to float a rumor than sink one.

Trouble hunters are not always trouble shooters.

Shoes only know if the stockings have holes.

Two things are hard on the heart—running up hill and running down people.

People will believe anything if whispered.

Before you give someone a piece of your mind, make sure you have enough to spare.

"She told me that you told her the secret I told you not to tell her." "Well, I told her not to tell you I told her." "Oh dear, in that case, don't you tell her I told you she told me."

Overheard: "I wouldn't say anything about her unless it's good, and boy, is this good!"

A man's tongue is an index to his mind.

In order to be a good fault finder one must be full of faults.

Something cracks every time a hot lie is put into a cold fact.

Man does not live by words alone although sometimes he has to eat them.—Adlai Stephenson.

The things you try to forget are the ones others try to remember.

The way to find out about a man is to ask him about another.

Don't use your tongue to cut your throat.

If you want to be heard—whisper.

A man must be *little* to *belittle*.

There is much difference between a busybody and a busy body.

MOTTO If you cannot say a good thing about a person, let's hear it.

Gossip is the art of saying nothing in such a way as to leave nothing unsaid.

It takes a *second-hand* person to deliver *first hand* gossip.

What Peter tells Paul tells more about Peter than Paul.

To make a long story short—don't tell it.

Some folks have *rumortism*.

Most things *too good to be true* aren't.

Those who use a tongue as their weapon will use their feet for defense.

He could hardly wait to hear what he was going to say.

So live where you can sell the family parrot to the town's gossip.

The tongue may be only 3 inches long, but it can ruin a man 6 feet high.

Gossips put two and two together and get twenty-two.

Old gossips are usually young flirts gone to seed.

Running down others has a way of catching up with us.

Be careful what you tell her—she is an "echo-maniac."

It is always better to wish you had said something than to wish you hadn't.

A gossip is one who burns the scandal at both ends.

HABIT

Habit is overcome only by habit.

Habit is like a soft bed—easy to get into but hard to get out of.

A great reward of hard work is sound sleep.

When you have a fight with your conscience and lose you won.

The men who move the world are the men the world cannot move.

Jesus didn't say, "Get ready", he said "Be ready."

The chains of habit are usually too small to be felt until they are too strong to be broken.

Baldness is not bad unless inside.

Religion is not just doing religious things, but doing all things religiously.

To make a man turn over a new leaf sometimes it is necessary to throw the book at him.

The man who just fiddles around will never get to lead the orchestra.

Respectable *vices* are doubly dangerous.

Strength unused becomes weakness.

Habit is a cable—we weave a thread of it every day, and at last cannot break it.

Work is man's most natural form of relaxation.

Good examples have twice the value of good advice.

The man who hungers and thirsts for righteousness will not come dragging in at meal time.

The best way to break a bad habit—drop it!

The man who minds his business usually has a good one.

Give your work your best and it will not get the best of you.

Garments of righteousness never go out of style.

Giving up sins is a lot easier than turning our back on sin.

The only man worse than a quitter is the man afraid to begin.

Going to bed can cure half the world's ills—and getting up the other half.

Tears of repentance are good for the eyes.

One can conquer a bad habit easier today than tomorrow.

If you hoot with the owls at night you cannot soar with the eagles in the morning.

HAPPINESS

Happiness is not a *buy-product*.

Joy is something that multiplies only when divided.

If you cannot find happiness along the way, you cannot find it at the end of the road.

When love empties the purse, happiness fills the heart.

Don't be so busy making your daily bread you forget to taste it.

Half our troubles come in wanting our way; the other half comes in getting it.

> Life itself can't give me joy,
> Unless I really will it;
> Life just gives me time and space,
> It's up to me to fill it.

All marriages are happy; it's the living together afterward that causes the trouble.

Could one buy happiness he would gripe at the price.

There are no answers to life in the back of the book.

Happiness can be thought, sought, taught, and caught but not bought.

You cannot borrow happiness but you can give it to others.

A smile is a light in the window of your face showing your heart is at home.

Be thankful if your dreams have not come true—neither have your nightmares.

Happiness is a perfume you cannot pour on others without getting a few drops yourself.

A smile is a gently curved line which sets a lot of things straight.

Hold your head up high but keep your nose at a friendly angle.

One advantage in traveling the strait and narrow way—no one is trying to pass you.

The trouble today is people want to reach the promised land without going through the wilderness.

The really happy man is one who can enjoy the scenery when on a detour.

In diving to the bottom of pleasures we bring up more rocks of sorrows than pearls of joy.

If you can't do what you like, try liking what you do.

Ulcers don't come by what you eat but what eats you.

A chip on the shoulder eventually becomes a heavy load.

It is not your position but your disposition that makes you happy.

Instead of broadcasting so much try tuning in.

A broken heart will not mend as long as it is worn on the sleeve.

Every minute you are angry you lose 60 seconds of happiness.

Doing nothing for others is the undoing of ourselves.—Mann

Happiness is made to be shared.

If there is a smile in your heart your face will show it.

The search for happiness is one of the chief sources of unhappiness.

Too many people who try to use the weekend to unwind simply unravel.

HOPE

Hope is a good breakfast but a bad supper.

An atheist has *reason* but no *hope* for his *reason*; a hypocrite has *hope* but no *reason*; a Christian has both *hope* and *reason*.

You have to keep your eyes open to make your dreams come true.

If we could only forget our troubles as we do our blessings.

There will be no crown-bearers in heaven who were not cross-bearers on earth.

If a man could have half his wishes he could double his trouble.

The best way out of a problem is through it.

REFORMER'S MOTTO: "No Thyself."

Without Christ, a hopeless end; with Christ an endless hope.

We need life in our hope to put hope in our lives.

Liberty is always dangerous, but it is the safest thing we have.

HUMOR

If you are quick on the draw, your bank balance will soon be shot.

"I always like to hear a man talk about himself, because then I never hear anything but good."—Will Rogers.

Church Bulletin Board: "You aren't too bad to come in; you are not too good to stay out."

Wouldn't it be great if people could see us as we see ourselves?

What does it matter which side our bread is buttered on—as long as we eat both sides?

A bank is an institution where you can borrow money as long as you can present evidence that you don't really need it.

Will electronic computers ever get smart enough to deny man made them?

Families used to be considered shiftless if they lived from payday to payday—now they wish they could!

Wealthy people miss one of the greatest thrills in life—making the last payment.

A fool with money to burn soon meets his match.

Money never made fools of anyone; it just shows 'em up.

Politics may make strange bed-fellows; they seemingly get used to the same bunk.

The safest way to double your money is to fold it and put it back in your pocket.

Now you can borrow enough to get out of debt!

Today's fashions are scriptural—"Lo and Behold."

A hamburger by any other name costs a lot more.

There is no fool like an old fool—you cannot beat experience.

Wisecracks are better from the wise than the cracks.

At today's prices it seems the nickel has gone the way of all buffaloes.

Sometimes a bad wisecrack outlasts a good sermon.

Every man has his price and every woman her figure.

If you could kick the fellow responsible for your problems you couldn't sit down in six months.

The man who loses his head is usually the last one to know it.

To err is human—to cover it up is too.

A boy smokes to prove he is a man; 20 years later he stops to prove the same thing.

> I like to hear the rooster crow;
>   He's like so many men I know.
> Who roar and rant and rave and shout,
>   And beat their manly chests,
>   Without a single thing to brag about.

Mrs. Blink: "So you've given up taking tranquilizers?"
Miss Blank: "Yes, I found myself being pleasant to people I
    shouldn't even speak to."

A man with a pet sin is like a boy with a dirty neck; neither wants to do anything about it.

At 50 a man feels his corns more than his oats.

There are better ways to get up in the world than by hitting the ceiling.

You can't reduce by talking about it; you have to keep your mouth shut.

If you're not afraid to face the music you may get to lead the band some day.

One of life's hardest jobs is to keep up the easy payments.

An antique may just be furniture paid for.

The 1960's will be known as the *Stoned Age*.

Fun is like life insurance—the older you get, the more it costs.

HANGOVER: What happens to a head not used the night before.

No man is so religiously sensitive as the self-made man when his creator is called into question.

How many apples were eaten in the Garden of Eden? Answer—11. Eve ate, Adam too, and the Devil won.

You never love anyone about whom you never laugh.

Some think they are big shots because they explode.

Most who slap us on the back want us to cough up something.

Hard work does not kill but it scares a lot of people half to death.

Tax is like golf—you drive hard to reach the green only to wind up in the hole.

All want to live long but none wish to get old.

A good laugh to a man is like oil to a machine.

Though the ant is famous for sticking to his job he still finds time to go to picnics.

The man who buys a cheap used car soon finds out how hard it is to drive a bargain.

Diet—penalty for exceeding the feed limit.

A weak moment with a bottle can mean several weeks in the jug.

Some who buy on time don't pay that way.

It is better to keep your mouth shut and be thought a fool than open it and remove all doubt.

Man is nothing but dust; some need to be settled.

Some think they have a good conscience; in reality it is a bad memory.

It is always the fresh eggs that get slapped in the pan.

Men used to show chivalry in street cars; now it is a standing joke.

When one dies of rabies, 1000's die of alcohol—so we shoot the dog and license the booze.

> I was drunk and in the gutter
> When a pig sat down to mutter.
> And a sober passer-by was heard to say
> You can tell a man who boozes
> By the company he chooses.
> And the dirty pig got up
> And walked away.

Women will not be equals of men until they can have a large bald spot on top of their heads and still think they are handsome.

If women aren't dangerous why do men always increase their insurance when they marry one!

Old hen to a bad chick, "If your father could see you now he would turn over in his gravy."

Too many calories add up to an awfully big future.

The fellow who thinks of nothing but "getting ahead" might possibly benefit from a new one.

If you think you have influence try ordering someone else's dog around.

Someone described a hypochondriac, "Even her swimming pool is pill-shaped."

Some women grow old before their time trying to look young after their time.

Did you hear about the jury that wouldn't convict the defendant—it didn't want to get involved.

JUDGING

The trouble with trying to *walk in the other fellow's shoes* is that they seldom fit.

A day's worry is harder than a week's work.

Too many go through life running from something that isn't after them.

Suspicion is worse than knowledge.

Hunt for good points in others; they must do the same for you.

It's hard to sling mud with clean hands.

Those at war with others are not at peace with themselves.

The faults of others are like headlights on an auto; they only seem more glaring than your own.

Plastic surgeons can do anything with a nose but keep it out of others' business.

Think too little of others and you will soon think too much of yourself.

Some find fault like it is buried treasure.

If you received 10¢ for kind words spoken about people and had to pay 5¢ for unkind ones how rich or poor would you be?

When God measures a man he places the tape around the heart, not the head.

A prejudice knows no logic.

The only exercise some get is jumping at conclusions, running down friends, sidestepping responsibilities, and pushing their luck.

A woman is not a good cook because she roasts her neighbors.

An egotist is always *me-deep* in conversation.

The most pointed remarks come from blunt people.

Strong and better words indicate a weak cause.

Some think they can push themselves forward by patting themselves on the back.

You cannot carve your way to success with a cutting tongue.

Don't worry about finding your station in life; someone will tell you where to get off.

When you think little of a person say as little as you think.

Minding your business is a full-time job.

Before we talk about another's fault—we should stop and count to ten—ten of our own.

The only folks to get even with are those who helped you.

Some men are like ink blotters—they soak it all up and get it backwards.

A Campbellite is a brook of false notions hatched from sectarian eggs and thrown into the faces of pure-minded Christians because misery loves company.

The elevator man is the only one with the right to run anyone down.

A narrow mind and a wide mouth are a dangerous combination.

You cannot white-wash yourself by blackening others.

A hole in the tooth seems large because the tongue is prone to exaggerate.

May I hold your highhorse while you dismount?

When your thoughts run riot your tongue is apt to join the crowd.

He has a right to criticize who has a heart to help.—Abraham Lincoln.

When two egotists meet, it is a case of an "I" for an "I."

Statistics are no substitute for judgment.

MARRIAGE

Making marriage work is like running a farm—you have to start all over each day.

The woman who arranges a match for her daughter wants to referee it too.

DIVORCE: price people pay for playing with matches.

The selection of a mate often determines whether one has 2 heavens or 2 hells.

Many girls who can dish it out cannot cook.

A charming woman without a heart can make a fool of a man without a head.

"I don't have any brothers or sisters," explained a Hollywood child, "but I have 3 fathers by my mother and 4 mothers by my father."

Marriages are made in heaven but maintenance work is done on earth.

Many a wife finds it is as hard to find a husband after marriage as before.

The only time some couples *hold hands* is when playing bridge.

Keeping husbands in hot water will not make them tender.

A man's success is a *nest egg* or *goose egg* according to the chick he married.

Marriages have trouble when one shows his *worst side* to his better half.

Psychology says girls marry men like their fathers—this explains why mothers cry at weddings.

Many men can read their wives like a book but cannot shut her up.

The magician who can saw a woman in half is no match for a husband who keeps his wife from flying to pieces.

Before marriage he talks and she listens; after marriage she talks and he listens; later they both talk and neighbors listen.

Marriage to some is like a violin; after the beautiful music is over the strings are still attached.

Husband looking into coffee cup, "There are enough grounds here for a divorce."

A wife with good horse sense never becomes a nag.

They are a perfect pair—she is a hypochondriac and he is a pill.

She used to knit for him—now she needles.

Don't trust your wife's judgment—look at whom she married!

The woman who thinks all men are beasts would give anything to be an animal trainer.

A lady needs to know four things—how to look like a girl, act like a lady, think like a man, and work like a dog.

Couples should remember the *we* comes before the *i* in *wedding*.

HONEYMOON: the short period between "I do" and "You'd better."

Many a couple is like a team of horses—separated by a tongue.

"Sometimes I think I married too young; I went straight from home work to house work."

Some wives can get money from their husbands with hardly *half-crying*.

Sometimes a marriage doesn't work because the wife has to.

A girl is not necessarily an artist just because she paints and chisels.

Observe the face of the wife to know her husband's character.

MARRIAGE: An investment that pays dividends if you pay interest.

Wives, like children, need to be loved most when they least deserve it.

The only way to understand a woman is to love her—and then it is not necessary to understand her.

A woman is usually afraid of a mouse, but she will usually take her chances with a wolf.

A suggestion for divorce reform—make the grounds for marriage tougher.

What the bride thinks coming down the aisle—"Aisle, Altar, Hymn."

Trial marriages? Whose isn't!

Wife to husband, "I took one of those compatibility tests in a magazine today and you flunked."

Love is the only game two can play and both win.

Many teenagers today just go ahead and marry, expecting their folks to be good supports about it.

NEGATIVISM

If you look back too much you will soon head that way.

There are 365 *Fear Nots* in the Bible—one for each day in the year.

Whether you believe you can do a thing or not, you are right.—Henry Ford.

Indecision is the death of good ideas.

Why not go out on the limb—that is where the fruit is.

Perhaps you cannot be a star—but you need not be a cloud.

In trying times—*TRY*.

Some have more objections than objectives.

Don't shoot a sparrow with a cannon!

Fear is the darkroom where negatives are developed.

Sometimes the best help conscience can get is cold feet.

Worry is interest paid on borrowed trouble.

What happens seldom bothers us as what might happen.

It is easier to tame a fanatic than put life in a corpse.

Even the lion has to defend himself against flies.

The *5* and *2* talent men took *14* words to explain success; the *1* talent man used *42* to explain failure.

Those frightened by the shadow of a doubt don't have a ghost of a chance.

When the going gets tough, the tough get going.

The hardest mountain climbing is to get out of a rut.

Those who gripe about the way the ball bounces are usually the ones who dropped it.

When you make your *mark* in the world watch out for guys with *erasers*.

Failure is the path of least persistence.

A bee without a sting makes no honey.

When you are kicked from the rear means you are ahead.

The cost of failure is greater than the price of success.

A man with a new idea is a crank until he succeeds.—Mark Twain.

Worry is interest paid on trouble before it came due.

Life is full of golden opportunities for what we do not want to do.

Henry Ford did not turn to experts for unbreakable glass— they knew too many reasons why it couldn't be done.

Nothing will ever be attempted if all possible objections must first be overcome.

Worries are mostly about tomorrow and yesterday.

The same jolt that moves little potatoes to the bottom moves the big ones to the top.

If God is your partner, make your plans larger.

A quitter never wins; a winner never quits.

Since you cannot completely eliminate the grapevine—use it.

Innovation is a gamble—but so is standing pat.

A penny will hide a star if you hold it close enough to your eyes.

Still water and still religion freeze the quickest.

You must lose a fly to catch a trout.

If there is no wind—*ROW*.

Those trying to do, yet fail, are much better than those who try to do nothing and succeed.

A cynic knows the price of everything and the value of nothing.

Indians mount horses from the right side—since the white man mounted from the left he figures this way was wrong!

Never give up! For 50 years they said the horse was through. Now look at him—a status symbol.

An optimist thinks this is a great world; a pessimist is afraid the optimist is right.

If you cannot win make the winner break a record!

The brook would lose its song if it lost its rocks.

He who cannot lead and will not follow at least makes a dandy roadblock.

No one can make you feel inferior without your consent.—E. Roosevelt.

Worrying about past events is like squeezing toothpaste back into the tube.

Don't stop a moving train because a dog barked.

The man rocking the boat is not at the oars.

Kites fly highest against the wind—not with it.

Worry gives little things long shadows.

There is no pain like that of a new idea.

Nothing worries a pessimist like an optimist who says there is nothing to worry about.

Real difficulties can be overcome; it is the imagined ones that are unconquerable.

Worry is a dog chasing his tail; remorse is when he catches it; despair is when he bites it off.

When I go to bed I leave my troubles in my clothes.

Anyone who doesn't worry today ought to have his TV set examined.

You don't have time to criticize when you harmonize, sympathize, and evangelize.

PRAYER

5 minutes on your knees is better than *50* minutes on a couch.

It is said of *667* prayers for specific things in the Bible there are *654* traceable answers.

If it is too small for prayer it is too small for burden.

If your problems are deep-seated and long-standing try kneeling.

I have lived to thank God all my prayers were not answered.

Christians and camels receive their burdens kneeling.

Courage is fear that has said its prayers.

If we hem in both ends of the day with prayer, it won't be so likely to unravel in the middle.

One of the fine things about silent prayer is that it shuts out the noise of the world.

A prayer that does not change us will not change God.

Life is fragile—handle with prayer.

Prayer requires more heart than tongue.

When your knees knock, kneel and pray.

God will not let anything happen to me that both of us cannot handle.

Seven prayerless days makes one weak.

A lot of kneeling keeps you in good standing.

If prayer does not remove the mountain then climb it.

There is more dignity in being on your knees than lying on a couch.

The only time you should beat anyone to his knees is in church.

Some sow wild oats six days then go to church on Sunday and pray for crop failure.

Prayer is a shield to the soul, a sacrifice to God, and a scourge to the devil.—Bunyan.

Look up and God will lift you up!

Some think God is like medicine; you do not need him when well.

If you do not open your windows to Jerusalem you will pitch your tent towards Sodom.

The successful sermon makes men pray. The successful prayer makes men work.

"Kneeology" will do more for the world than "theology."

Regardless of your position in life, getting on your knees will help keep you on your toes.

Praying without praising is kneeling without feeling.

Prayerless pews make powerless pulpits.

Man is often disappointed when his small prayers are not answered; God is always disappointed when man's prayers are too small.

If you ain't got no problems then prayer ain't got no suction.

"Dear God, give me patience—and I want it right now."

In the school of prayer there are many promotions but no graduations.

You cannot expect a million dollar answer to a ten cent prayer.

Most people make the same mistake with God they do with people—they do all the talking.

PREACHERS

It is futile for a minister to drum up trade during the week unless he is prepared to deliver the goods on Sunday.

Preaching fails that only *charms* not *changes.*

It is not our job to make the gospel *acceptable* but *available—* not make them like it but see that they get it.

> I do not see my preacher's eyes,
> However bright they shine;
> For when he prays, he closes his
> And when he preaches, closes mine.

The world needs more sermons in shoes.

Don't worry about the *Far Left* or *Far Right.* Worry about the *High Above* and the *Way Below.*

If you want a revival get on fire; the people will come to see the fire.—Wesley.

If you cannot fill the pulpit, fill the pews.

God had only one begotten son and He made of him a preacher.

A good preacher scratches where members don't itch.

There is no use in walking anywhere to preach if we do not preach as we walk.

You will never be a better teacher of the Bible than you are a student of it.

Preachers prefer holding services with you than over you.

If you have scorn for pastoral work get out of the pulpit.

Preachers are determined—if they don't get on your toes they get in your hair.

If the sermon pricks the conscience, it must have had some good points.

If you need an excuse see the preacher—he has heard more than anyone.

Some brethren not only want only spiritual milk they want it *pastorized.*

The preacher who takes a *look* at the world will have members who take a *step* toward it.

A sermon is not to be liked but to be lived.

Some preachers need no introductions—they need conclusions.

The preacher who does not broaden and deepen his sermons ends up lengthening them.

Overheard, "He's got a lot of depth on the surface, but way down deep he is awfully shallow."

A poor listener seldom hears a good sermon.

The preacher who knows what he is talking about can afford to use words everyone understands.

PROVERBS

Men do not stumble over mountains but molehills.

A foolish man is like a button—always popping off at the wrong time.

Man who beefs too much finds himself in stew.

Ask an atheist after a good meal if he believes in a cook.

Hypocrisy is the homage vice pays to virtue.

American ends in "I Can."

Too many trains of thoughts have too many *loco motives*.

A loose tongue gets into tight places.

Praise makes a good man better and a bad man worse.

Tact is the ability to close your mouth before someone wants to.

The thoughtless are seldom wordless.

If there were no difficulties there would be no triumphs.

Give everyone your ear but few your tongue.

A man is not bright because he burns the candle at both ends.

If you don't wish to be shown up—don't show off.

It is much easier to take the credit for something you didn't do than the blame for something you did.

The worst indigestion comes in eating your own words.

Actually, there's only a slight difference in keeping your chin up and sticking your neck out—but you'd better know the difference.

Seven days of indulgence makes one *WEAK!*

The man with push will pass the man with pull.

Common sense is uncommon.

A candle loses no light in lighting another.

A flatterer says things to your face he wouldn't dare say to your back.

One's judgment can be no better than his information.

He who rolls up his sleeves seldom loses his shirt.

Leisure is good but boredom is its brother.

Inspiration without perspiration ends in frustration.

When we allow little men to cast long shadows it is nearly sunset.—George Bailey.

Use your head—it is the little thing that counts.

He who falls in love with self has no rivals.—B. Franklin.

He who wants a bed of roses must put in much spade work.

The depth of one's convictions measures the breadth of his influence.

It is nice to be important but more important to be nice.

The entrances to trouble are wide—the exits narrow.

No man is a complete loss—he may be used as a horrible example.

The clock passes time by keeping its hands busy.

Killing time is not murder—it is suicide.

He who burns candle at both ends will go out like a light.

Too many necessities is the mother of tension.

He who wants to open the door of opportunity must push.

The way to avoid trouble is to wrong no man and write no woman.

It is hard for an empty rack to stand up right.

Anger is the wind that blows out the light of intelligence.

Those who have free seats at the play hiss first.—Chinese.

Lord, save me from the gnats, I can take care of the elephants.

He who rides hobby wants whole road to himself.

Any government big enough to give you everything you want is big enough to take everything you have.

He who thinketh by the inch and talketh by the yard deserveth to be kicked by the foot.

People who get down to brass tacks usually rise rapidly.

An atheist is a person with no *invisible* means of support.

The wheels of progress are not turned by cranks.

Better keep yourself bright and clean; you are the window through which you see the world.—G. B. Shaw.

When in deep water, keep your mouth shut.

Beware the fury of a patient man.

He who makes most noise about problem does least about it.

To handle yourself use your head; to handle others use your heart.

The wind pushes only those who have set their sails.

It is good to have ability, but the ability to discover ability in others is the true test.

FOR SALE: A bladeless knife without a handle.

He who listens to others' advice soon makes others' mistakes.

Example is a language all men can read.

Good intentions don't help a man traveling the wrong road.

People who fly into a rage always make a bad landing.

Courtesy is contagious; start an epidemic.

Every heel needs a sock.

A green employee is better than a blue one.

If your *morals* must go *down* to get *up* in society you'd better stay on the *level.*

The Great Physician never wrote a wrong prescription.

Peace conferences fail like revivals fail—those who ought to attend aren't there.

A bad tooth and your conscience have one thing in common—they won't hurt nearly so bad if you will keep your mouth shut.

An uneasy conscience makes a restless night.

Where law ends, tyranny begins.

An ounce of doing is worth a pound of intention.

When we forget ourselves we do things that will be remembered.

An upright man can never be a downright failure.

A wilful waste makes a woeful want.

A useless life is an early death.

The man whose ship has come in will find relatives waiting at the dock.

A hypocrite is a person "white-washed" rather than "washed -white."

You cannot sharpen a knife on a feather pillow.

Do not become broadminded from shallow thinking.

People who rely on pull are pushing their luck.

Civil rights are not an excuse for civil wrongs.

People who fall at your feet may be reaching for the rug.

The longer a man is wrong, the surer he is he's right.

Tact is the ability to give a person a shot in the arm without his feeling the needle.

The milk of human kindness never curdles.

Some of our books are so "down-to-earth" they should be "plowed under."

The main objection to old age is that there is no future in it.

Instead of "putting others in their place" put yourself in their place.

The older a man gets the better he could swim as a boy.

SUCCESS

Luck is a lazy man's estimate of a hard worker's success.

Evil often triumphs but it can never conquer.

Opportunity would be easier to spot if it didn't come disguised as hard work.

No man is small who does a small job in a big way.

If you worry about what people think of you, it means you have more confidence in their opinions than yours.

Some of us don't know what we want, but we are sure we don't have it.

After all is said and done more is said than done.

When your work speaks for itself, don't interrupt.

The world is full of people making a good living but poor lives.

Heads, hearts, and hands could settle the world's problems better than arms.

Success makes failures out of too many people.

A man who is on a wild goose chase all his life never feathers much of a nest.

The road to success is always under construction.

People who talk like *big wheels* are just spokesmen.

The future is written in the past for those with the skill to read.

Footprints left in the sands of time were made by work shoes.

A diamond is just a piece of coal that stuck to its job.

Big shots are little shots who kept shooting.

The greatest pleasure is to do a good deed in secret and have it found out by accident.

God tries you with a little to see what you could do with a lot.

All success is relative—the more success, the more relatives.

Success that is just out of our reach keeps us on our toes.

When success turns a man's head, it always leaves him looking the wrong way.

Luck is the idol of the idle.

Two kinds of men never succeed—those who cannot do what they are told and those who cannot do anything else.

You cannot climb the ladder of success with your hands in your pocket.

Although there is much room at the top there is none to sit down.

He who only works for pay will be dissatisfied with the returns.

People cannot walk over you until you lie down.

Scandal, crime, failure make news —but success makes history.

Man is pulled between wanting to be God and be with God.

Big trouble with the ladder of success—no one is there to hold it for you.

The first thing needed to make a dream come true is to wake up.

Paderewski, the great pianist, said, "Before I was a master, I was a slave."

There is only one place you can find success without work—in your dictionary.

Success is getting what you want; happiness is wanting what you get.—Dale Carnegie

Folks who never do more than they get paid for never get paid for any more than they do.

Success is 1% inspirational and 99% perspirational.

TOMORROW

Kindness planned for tomorrow doesn't count today.

Vision is the art of seeing things invisible.

NOW is the word appearing upon each page of the Bible.

What we find depends upon what we look for.

When they congratulate your looking young they figure you are old.

Life can only be understood backwards; but it must be lived forwards.

There can be no rainbow without a cloud and storm.

You can take the day off, but you cannot put it back.

Tomorrow is purchased today.

The best thing about the future—it only comes one day at a time.

Time heals many wounds; it also wounds many heels.

How easy it is the night before to get up early the next morning.

Today's mighty oak is yesterday's little nut that held his ground.

You do not waste time; time wastes you.

The past is valuable as a guide post but not a hitching post.

The best way to get rid of the past is to do something about the future.

How we use today determines how tomorrow uses us.

Today is the tomorrow you worried about yesterday.

To be the man of the hour make every minute count.

Tomorrow is a promissory note; yesterday a canceled check.

It's easier to persuade people to *do better* tomorrow than be their best today.

When the day is done you frequently discover that not much is.

If it took effort to go from today to tomorrow many would still be yesterday.

Counting time is not as important as making time count.

The best thing to save for old age is yourself.

Worry doesn't eliminate tomorrow from its griefs but it does empty today of its joys.

Worry is seldom on time—it is usually too early and too late.

Some people have three kinds of trouble—all they have had, all they have now, and all they expect to have.

Today you speak; Tomorrow you hear the echo of your voice.

When we forget ourselves we do things that will be remembered.

An upright man can never be a downright failure.

The duty of many should not be the task of the few.

Good intentions, like crying babies, should be carried out.

Success is never permanent; neither is failure.

The employee who watches the clock will always be one of the hands.

Failure should be our teacher—not our undertaker.

Things done for effect are seldom effective.

What kind of test is it where no one can fail?

Some reach the top of the ladder only to find it is leaning against the wrong wall.

Success comes from having the proper aim as well as the right ammunition.

Tomorrow is often the most busy day of the year.

It is not only later than you think—it is sooner than you suspect.

The future frightens only those who prefer living in the past.

The man who knows why he is here is pretty sure to have a fair idea of where he is going.

It is the business of the future to be dangerous.

TRUTH

Error will slip through a crack while the truth will stick in a doorway.—H. W. Shaw.

The mind is like a parachute—it works only when open.

Truth doesn't hurt unless it ought to.

Mud thrown is ground lost.

Too often truth is treated anatomically, like a corpse in pickle to be dissected.

A sure way to stop a *red-hot* argument? Lay a *cold fact* on it.

Many are willing to be generous who will not be just; generosity, thusly, becomes the price of justice.

Truth, like oil in water, always rises to the top.

Hell is truth found too late.

It is easy to forgive a child afraid of the dark; the real tragedy is men afraid of the light.—Plato.

Beware half truths—you may have the wrong half!

Some throw away a bushel of truth because it has a grain of error. Others swallow a bushel of error because it contains a grain of truth.

Being ignorant is not as bad as being unwilling to learn.

Don't think your Bible is dry inside because it is dusty outside.

No man has good enough memory to be a successful liar.

Wisdom is only found in truth.

The Bible is vascular; no matter where you prick it—it bleeds.

The foolish and the dead never change their opinion.

Half the lies you hear nowadays are not true!

Too many mistake looking for seeing, listening for hearing, observation for understanding, and opinions for thinking.

The man who only samples the Bible infrequently will not develop a taste for it.

Acts should follow facts.

No man ever got lost on a straight road.—Lincoln.

A lie has short legs; truth will overtake it.

When you tell the truth you don't have to remember what you said.

Everyone wants truth on their side but few want to be on the side of truth.

The Bible is the most wonderful book I never read.

A chapter a day helps keep the devil away.

A Bible in the hand is better than 2 on the shelf.

The truth needs no crutches; if it limps it is a lie.

The liar's punishment is not his being disbelieved but his disbelieving all others.

Sin has many tools, but a lie is the handle that fits them all.

Men seek the truth—not because it is lost but they are.

Men do not reject the Bible because it contradicts itself but because it contradicts them.

Truth, like oil in water, will eventually come to the surface.

It does no good to paint the pump if the water is poisoned.

Never put a question mark where God put a period.

He who closes his eyes cannot walk a straight line.

Do not treat truth as fiction or fiction as truth.

The more you speak of yourself, the more you are apt to lie.

Nothing ruins truth like stretching it.

Too often we seek justice for "just us."

WISDOM

The biggest fraud is to cheat yourself.

We are such little men when the stars come out.

One starts cutting his wisdom tooth when he bites off more then he can chew.

Men tire themselves in pursuit of rest.

The best way to get ahead is to have one.

Live spelled backwards is evil.

When met by temptation, turn to the right.

Good judgment comes from experience and experience from poor judgment.

Flattery is like perfume—smell it but do not swallow it.

You will find no statues to committees.

If you have castles in the air put a foundation under them.

A man afraid of work must be brave enough to meet poverty.

Very few people find a sermon long if it is helpful.

One step does not make a walk.

A chain of thought is no stronger than its weakest think.

Most had rather be ruined with praise than saved with criticism.

The dog with the bone is always in danger.

Some men grow—others swell.

Man is like water—in that he seeks his own level.

The devil is author of both religious differences and religious indifference.

Don't brag—it isn't the whistle that pulls the train.

Every time you speak your mind is on parade.

Prepare and prevent, rather than repair and repent.

The emptier the pot, the quicker it boils.

Half-knowledge is worse than ignorance.

Many think where they should feel and feel where they should think.

Where a man goes hereafter depends on what he goes after here.

Fools make prophecies; wise men make plans.

Sometimes an argument only proves two people are present.

Sometimes problems are harder to face than solve.

It takes years to find a reputation lost in a minute.

Prejudice is being down on something you are not up on.

Big things are done by big men who didn't have the time to do them.

Anger is one letter short of *danger*.

Small ills are the fountains
Of most of our groans;
Men trip not on mountains—
They stumble on stones.
(Chinese)

An honest day's work is natures' tranquilizer.

If you expect a place in the sun, you will have to get blisters.

Flattery is like some medicine; it should not be taken internally.

The most difficult thing to open is a closed mind.

Do not argue with a fool—the bystanders may not know which one is which.

The H-bomb will never prove who is right but who is left.

Mental cases hardest to cure are those who are crazy about themselves.

107

Horse sense is stable thinking.

Often when the conscience tries to speak it finds the line busy.

People who straddle the fence never do any plowing.

When the majority in a democracy are insane the sane go to the asylum.

He who stands in the rain is bound to get wet.

Tact fails the moment it is noticed.

Wise men learn more from fools than fools from wise men.

Look for the humor in the serious, the joy in the sad, the strength in the weak, and the best in the bad.

Righteous indignation is often nothing more than self-righteous irritation.

Watch your step; everyone else does.

Silence is sometimes golden; sometimes plain yellow.

If you don't learn from mistakes there is no sense in making them.

Living without faith is like driving in a fog.

WORSHIP

Worship is to a Christian what a mainspring is to a watch.

Human eyes are never as clear as when washed by tears.

Too many try to get something from worship without putting something in.

Organize the day around your duty to God.

You put life into religion by putting religion into life.

THE GOSPEL ACCORDING TO YOU

There's a Gospel according to Matthew:
    To Mark and to Luke and John, too.
There's another that many are reading—
    The Gospel according to you.
All teachings we find in the Bible
    Are but facts we believe to be true:
You must live them to make them the Gospel—
    The Gospel according to you.
Many read not the words of the Bible;
    I will tell you what some of them do—
They are reading the book you are writing—
    The Gospel according to you.
There's power in the minister's preaching;
    So you say, I believe this is true;
But the thing that may tell most on others
    Is the Gospel according to you.
God help you to Christ to be faithful,
    And to live all his teachings so true,
So that all may be seeing his spirit
    In the Gospel according to you.